It's all down hill when

To enjoy your speci...

This book will help you

Maintain a smooth marriage.

Gary 6-10-1998

Australia, Adelaide.

Design: Jill Coote

Recipes: Mridula Baljekar

Recipe Photography: Peter Barry

Recipe styling: Bridgeen Deery and Wendy Devenish

Jacket and Illustration Artwork: Jane Winton,

courtesy of Bernard Thornton Artists, London

Compiled and introduced by Laura Potts

Edited by Josephine Bacon

Published by
CHARTWELL BOOKS, INC.
A Division of **BOOK SALES, INC.**
110 Enterprise Avenue
Secaucus, New Jersey 07094

CLB 3357

© 1993 CLB Publishing,

Godalming, Surrey, England

Printed and bound in Singapore

ISBN 1-55521-984-5

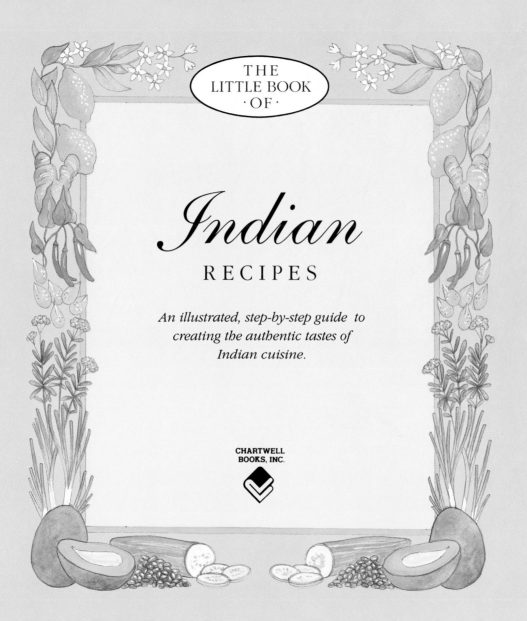

THE
LITTLE BOOK
· OF ·

Indian

RECIPES

*An illustrated, step-by-step guide to
creating the authentic tastes of
Indian cuisine.*

CHARTWELL
BOOKS, INC.

Introduction

India is a huge country and its regions were, until recently, very isolated, with poor systems of transport hampering communication. This isolation is reflected in the regional nature of Indian cuisine. Each region made use of the foods that grew locally, particularly spices, and dishes from certain areas developed their own unique characteristics and flavours.

Other factors, aside from regionalism, have influenced the development of Indian cuisine. Over the centuries India has been invaded by many nations, each of which has made a contribution to the style of cookery. The Persian influence, brought to India by the invading Mughals, is particularly marked in northern India, where the dishes are characterized by their delicate flavors and smooth sauces. These textures and tastes are achieved by the addition of coconut and milk or cream, and the use of dried fruits and nuts. The Kashmiris, too, made a notable contribution with their use of saffron, and other rare spices. Persian, Greek, Roman, Mongol, Portuguese and British are among the many other cultures that have both given to and learned from the cookery of India.

It is almost impossible to separate the development of Indian cuisine from the religious influences that have shaped the nation. Muslims, for instance, are prohibited from eating pork, and the

consumption of beef is strictly forbidden to Hindus, as the cow is thought of as a sacred animal. Indeed, high caste Hindus in many parts of India are bound by their religion to be vegetarian.

Yet, despite such obvious differences, similar attitudes to food are prevalent throughout India. A selection of dishes is usually served at an Indian meal and these are accompanied by a variety of breads and rice. Traditionally, six *rasas* or flavors – sweet, salty, bitter, astringent, sour and pungent – should be included in every meal. Each of these flavors is believed to have a health benefit of its own, and should be included in a meal in a specific ratio to the other flavors. Indian cooks have long recognized that spices have a value beyond merely flavoring food, and have used these properties to full effect. Spices have a place in Indian cookery both as appetite stimulators and as digestives. Great care, however, is taken to ensure that the spices used in cooking complement rather than overpower each other.

The recipes in this book cover some of the principal styles of Indian cooking, and give an introduction to the techniques needed to create them. The carefully selected recipes reflect the Indian love of food and give you ideas of how to create and serve authentic Indian dishes.

Chicken Tikka

The recipe for this popular favorite has been adapted for the conventional oven.

PREPARATION: 30-35 mins, plus time to marinate
COOKING: 15-18 minutes

---

1 pound boneless, skinned chicken breast
1 tsp salt
Juice of ½ a lemon
½ tsp annatto color or a few drops of red food
    coloring mixed with 1 tbsp tomato paste
2 cloves garlic, peeled and coarsely chopped
½-inch ginger root, peeled and chopped
2 tsps ground coriander (cilantro)
½ tsp ground allspice or garam masala
¼ of a whole nutmeg, finely grated
½ tsp ground turmeric
⅔ cup thick set plain yogurt
4 tbsps corn or vegetable oil
½ tsp chili powder

---

1. Cut the chicken into 1-inch cubes. Sprinkle with ½ tsp salt and the lemon juice – mix well, cover and set aside 30 minutes.

2. Put the remaining ingredients into a liquidizer and blend until smooth.

3. Sieve this marinade over the chicken pieces with the back of a metal spoon until only a very coarse mixture is left.

4. Coat the chicken thoroughly with the sieved marinade. Cover and leave to marinate 6-8 hours or overnight in the refrigerator.

Step 7 Thread the chicken onto skewers, leaving ¼ inch gap between each piece.

5. Preheat the oven to 450°F.

6. Line a roasting pan with aluminum foil.

7. Thread the chicken onto skewers, leaving ¼-inch gap between each piece.

8. Place the skewers in the prepared roasting pan and brush with some of the remaining marinade.

9. Cook in the oven 6-8 minutes.

10. Take the pan out of the oven, turn the skewers over and brush the pieces of chicken with the remaining marinade.

11. Return the pan to the oven and cook a further 6-8 minutes.

12. Shake off any excess liquid from the chicken.

13. Place the skewers on a serving platter.

Vegetable Samosas

MAKES 18

Vegetable Samosas are a popular Indian snack.

PREPARATION: 60 mins
COOKING: 60 mins

1 pound potatoes
2 tbsps cooking oil
½ tsp black mustard seeds
1 tsp cumin seeds
2 dried red chilies, coarsely chopped
1 medium-sized onion, finely chopped
1-2 fresh green chilies, chopped and seeded
½ tsp ground turmeric
1 tsp ground coriander
1 tsp ground cumin
1 tsp salt or to taste
1 tbsp chopped coriander (cilantro) leaves

Pastry
2 cups all-purpose flour
4 tbsp ghee (clarified butter) or butter, melted
½ tsp salt
5 tbsp warm water
Oil for frying

1. Boil the potatoes in their skins, allow to cool thoroughly, then peel and dice them.

2. Heat the oil and add mustard seeds. As soon as they start crackling, add the cumin seeds and red chilies, and then the onions and green chilies. Saute till the onions are soft. Add the turmeric, coriander, and cumin.

3. Add the potatoes and the salt. Reduce heat to

Step 9 Fill the cones, leaving about ¼-inch border on the top.

low, stir and cook until thoroughly mixed.

4. Remove from heat and add coriander leaves.

5. Add the butter and salt to the flour. Rub in well.

6. To make the dough, mix the flour and water. Knead until the dough feels soft. Divide the dough into 9 balls. Rotate each ball between your palms in a circular motion, then press it down to make a flat cake.

7. Roll out each flat cake into 4-inch disks and cut into two. Use each semicircle of pastry as one envelope.

8. Moisten the straight edge with a little warm water. Fold the semicircle of pastry in half to form a triangular cone. Join the straight edges by pressing them hard into each other.

9. Fill these cones with the potato mixture, leaving about ¼-inch border on the top. Moisten the top edges and press them together.

10. Deep-fry the samosas until golden-brown.

Spiced Potato Bites

SERVES 6-8

Delicious sautéed potatoes flavored with a light sprinkling of spices.

PREPARATION: 30 mins
COOKING: 10-12 mins

1½ pounds potatoes
4 tbsps oil
½ tbsp salt
¼ tsp garam masala
½ tsp ground cumin
½ tsp ground coriander
¼-½ tsp chili powder

1. Boil the potatoes in their skins, cool thoroughly, peel, and dice them into 1-inch cubes.

Step 1 Peel and dice the cooked potatoes.

Step 3 Brown the potatoes evenly, stirring them occasionally.

2. In a wide, shallow skillet, preferably non-stick or cast iron, heat the oil over medium heat. It is important to have the right pan otherwise the potatoes will stick.

3. Add the potatoes and spread them evenly around the pan. Brown the potatoes evenly, stirring them occasionally.

4. When the potatoes are brown, sprinkle with the salt, garam masala, cumin, coriander, and the chili powder. Stir gently and mix until the potatoes are fully coated with the spices. Remove from the heat.

Fish Bhoona

SERVES 4

For a successful bhoona the spices must be fried until they are a rich brown color.

PREPARATION: 15-20 mins
COOKING: 30-35 mins

1½ pounds fish steaks
6 tbsps cooking oil

Mix the following 4 ingredients in a small bowl
1 tbsp all-purpose flour
¼ tsp ground turmeric
¼ tsp chili powder
¼ tsp salt

1 large onion, coarsely chopped
½-inch ginger root, peeled and chopped
2-4 cloves garlic, peeled and coarsely chopped
½ tsp ground turmeric
¼ tsp chili powder
1 tsp ground coriander
½ tsp garam masala or curry powder
1 small can of tomatoes
⅔ cup warm water
½ cup frozen garden peas
1 tsp salt
1 tbsp chopped coriander (cilantro) leaves

1. Skin the fish, wash and dry thoroughly, and cut into 1 × 2-inch pieces.

2. Heat 2 tbsps of the oil in a large skillet, preferably nonstick, over medium heat.

3. Lightly dust the fish in the seasoned flour and place in the hot oil. Adjust heat to medium-

Step 1 Cut the fish into 1 × 2-inch pieces.

high. Fry the fish until all the pieces are evenly browned. Drain on absorbent paper.

4. Put the onion, ginger, and garlic into a liquidizer and blend until smooth.

5. Heat the remaining oil over medium heat, add the onion mixture, and stir. Heat through, then turn heat down. Fry 3-4 minutes.

6. Add the turmeric, chili, coriander, and garam masala and fry 4-5 minutes, stirring continuously. During this time add 1 tbsp juice from the tomatoes at a time to prevent the spices from sticking to the skillet.

7. Now add one tomato at a time, along with any remaining juice. Cook until the tomato is well incorporated into the rest of the ingredients.

8. Add the water, peas, and salt. Bring to the boil and add the fish. Cover and simmer for 5 minutes, then remove from heat. Garnish with coriander leaves.

YUM! YUM!

Fish Shahjahani

SERVES 4

Fried Brown Rice makes the ideal accompaniment for this rich fish dish.

PREPARATION: 15 mins
COOKING: 15-20 mins

1½ pounds fillet of any white fish
⅓ cup roasted cashews
½ cup single cream
4 tbsps unsalted butter
1 large onion, finely sliced
2-inch piece of cinnamon stick, broken up
4 green cardamom pods, split open
2 whole cloves
1-2 fresh green chilies, sliced lengthwise
1 tsp ground turmeric
¾ cup warm water
1 tsp salt
1 tbsp lemon juice

1. Rinse the fish gently in cold water, dry on absorbent paper and cut into 1 × 2-inch pieces.

2. Put the cashews and the cream in an electric blender and blend to a reasonably fine mixture.

3. In a wide, shallow skillet melt the butter over medium heat and fry onions, cinnamon, cardamom, cloves, and green chilies until the onions are lightly browned. Stir in the turmeric.

4. Add the water and salt and arrange the fish in a single layer. Bring to the boil, cover the pan, and simmer 2-3 minutes.

Step 3 Fry onions, cinnamon, cardamom, cloves, and green chilies until the onions are lightly browned.

5. Now add the cashew-and-cream mixture and stir gently until the pieces of fish are well coated. Cover the pan again and simmer a further 2-3 minutes.

6. Remove from heat and gently stir in the lemon juice. Remove cinnamon pieces before serving.

Step 5 Add the cashew-and-cream mixture and stir gently until the pieces of fish are well covered.

Kheema-Palak (Ground Meat with Spinach)

SERVES 4-6

Ground meat with spinach is a popular Indian dish.

PREPARATION: 15-20 mins
COOKING: 40 mins

4 tbsps oil
½ tsp black mustard seeds
1 tsp cumin seeds
1 fresh green chili, finely chopped (seeded if a
 milder flavor is preferred)
1-inch ginger root, peeled and finely grated
6 garlic cloves, peeled and crushed
1 pound lean ground lamb or beef
1 large onion, finely sliced
2 cinnamon sticks, 2-inches long each, broken up
½ tsp ground turmeric
1 tbsp ground cumin
½ tsp ground black pepper
2 cups fresh chopped spinach or 1 cup frozen
 spinach, defrosted and drained
1 cup canned tomatoes, drained and chopped
1 tsp garam masala or curry powder

1. Heat half the oil in a wide, shallow skillet over medium heat and fry the mustard seeds until they crackle. Add the cumin seeds and immediately follow with the green chili, ginger, and half the garlic. Stir and fry 30 seconds.

2. Add the ground meat, stir and fry until all

Step 3 Add the onions and cinnamon sticks and fry until the onions are lightly browned.

the liquid evaporates – this will take 8-10 minutes. Remove the pan from the heat.

3. In a separate skillet, heat the remaining oil over medium heat and stir in the rest of the garlic. Add the onions and cinnamon sticks, and fry until the onions are lightly browned.

4. Adjust heat to low and add the turmeric, cumin, and black pepper. Stir and fry 1 minute. Add the spinach and mix thoroughly.

5. Add the ground meat and stir until the spinach and the meat are thoroughly mixed. Cover the pan and simmer 15 minutes.

6. Adjust heat to medium, add 1 tsp salt and the tomatoes, stir and cook for 2-3 minutes.

7. Add the garam masala, stir and cook for a further 2-3 minutes. Remove the pan from heat.

Coriander Chicken

SERVES 4-6

Coriander Chicken is the perfect choice for any dinner party menu.

PREPARATION: 20 mins, plus time to marinate
COOKING: 45-50 mins

2¼ pounds chicken parts, skinned
2-4 cloves garlic, peeled and crushed
⅔ cup thick set plain yogurt
5 tbsps cooking oil
1 large onion, finely sliced
2 tbsps ground coriander (cilantro)
½ tsp ground black pepper
1 tsp ground mixed spice
½ tsp ground turmeric
½ tsp cayenne pepper or chili powder
½ cup warm water
1 tsp salt
2 tbsps ground almonds
2 hard-cooked eggs, sliced
¼ tsp paprika

---

1. Cut each chicken part in two, mix thoroughly with the crushed garlic, and the

Step 1 Cut each chicken part into two, mix thoroughly with the crushed garlic, and the yogurt.

Step 4 Adjust heat to medium-high and fry the chicken 5-6 minutes until it changes color.

yogurt. Cover the container and leave to marinate in a cool place for 2-4 hours or overnight in the refrigerator.

2. Heat the oil over medium heat and sauté the onions until they are golden brown. Remove with a slotted spoon and keep aside.

3. In the same oil, fry the coriander, ground pepper, ground mixed spice, and turmeric 15 seconds and add the chicken along with all the marinade in the container.

4. Adjust heat to medium-high and fry the chicken for 5-6 minutes until it turns color.

5. Add the cayenne or chili powder, water, salt, and the fried onion slices. Bring to the boil, cover the pan, and simmer 30 minutes until the chicken is tender.

6. Stir in the ground almonds and remove from heat. Garnish with the slices of egg and paprika.

Shahi Korma

SERVES 4-6

This dish is rich and creamy and is a perfect choice for a special occasion.

PREPARATION: 20-25 mins
COOKING: 1 hr 30 mins

2¼ pounds boned leg of lamb, trimmed and cut
  into 1½-inch cubes
⅔ cup thick set plain yogurt
½-inch root ginger, peeled and grated
3-4 cloves of garlic, peeled and crushed
2 tbsps ghee (clarified butter) or unsalted butter
2 medium-sized onions, finely chopped

Grind the following ingredients
2 tbsps coriander seeds
8 green cardamom pods
10 whole black peppercorns
3-4 dried red chilies
1 tsp cinnamon
1 tsp mace

3-4 tbsps chopped fresh mint
2 tbsps ground almonds
1¼ cups warm water
½ tsp saffron strands, crushed
2 tbsps raw split cashews
⅔ cup single cream
1 tbsp rosewater

1. Put the meat, yogurt, ginger, and garlic into
a bowl. Mix thoroughly, cover and leave to
marinate 2-4 hours.

2. Put the marinated meat, along with any

Step 1 Put the meat into a bowl and add the yogurt, ginger and garlic.

marinade, in a heavy-based saucepan. Bring to
a slow simmer, cover and cook 45-50 minutes
stirring occasionally. Transfer the meat to
another container and keep hot.

3. Melt the ghee and fry the onions.

4. Lower heat and add the ground ingredients
and the mint; stir and fry 2-3 minutes. Add half
of the liquid in which the meat was cooked, stir
and cook 1-2 minutes. Add the ground almonds
and the remaining meat broth, stir and cook for
1-2 minutes.

5. Adjust heat to medium and add the meat.
Stir and fry the meat 5-6 minutes.

6. Add water, saffron, 1-1/2 tsp salt, and the
cashews, bring to a slow boil, cover and
simmer 20 minutes.

7. Add the cream, stir and mix well. Simmer
uncovered for 6-8 minutes. Stir in the rosewater
and remove from the heat.

Meat Madras

SERVES 4-6

This hot curry is named after Madras, the major city in southern India.

PREPARATION: 25-30 mins
COOKING: 1 hr 20 mins

6 tbsps cooking oil
2 medium onions, coarsely chopped
1-inch root ginger, peeled and coarsely chopped
3-4 cloves garlic, peeled and coarsely chopped
4-6 dried red chilies
2 large cloves garlic, peeled and crushed
1-2 fresh green chilies, sliced lengthwise
1 cup canned tomatoes
3 tsps ground cumin
1 tsp ground coriander
½-1 tsp chili powder
1 tsp ground turmeric
2¼ pounds leg or shoulder of lamb, fat trimmed, cut into 1½-inch cubes
¾ cup warm water
1¼ tsps salt
1 tsp garam masala or curry powder

1. Heat 3 tbsps oil over medium heat and sauté the onions, ginger, garlic, and red chilies until the onions are soft, stirring frequently. Remove from heat and allow to cool.

2. Meanwhile, heat the remaining oil over medium heat, and fry the crushed garlic and green chilies until the garlic is lightly browned.

Step 7 Blend the onion mixture and add to the meat.

3. Add half the tomatoes, along with the juice; stir and cook for 1-2 minutes.

4. Add the cumin, coriander, chili powder, and turmeric, adjust heat to low and cook 6-8 minutes, stirring frequently.

5. Add the meat and adjust heat to medium-high. Stir and fry 5-6 minutes until meat turns color.

6. Add the water, bring to the boil, cover, and simmer for 30 minutes.

7. Place the fried onion mixture in an electric blender and add the remaining tomatoes. Blend until smooth and add this to the meat - bring to the boil, add salt, and mix well. Cover the pan and simmer further 35-40 minutes or until the meat is tender.

8. Stir in the garam masala and remove from heat.

Chapatties

MAKES 14

A chapatti is a dry-roasted, unleavened bread best eaten as soon as it is cooked.

PREPARATION: 20-25 mins
COOKING: 35-40 mins

3 cups fine wholewheat flour
½ tsp salt
1 tbsp butter, or ghee
¾ cup-1¼ cups warm water
1 tbsp extra flour in a shallow bowl or plate

1. Food Mixer Method: Place the flour, salt, and fat together in the bowl and mix thoroughly at medium-to-low speed, taking care to see that all the fat has been broken up and well incorporated into the flour. Turn speed down to minimum and gradually add the water. When the dough is formed, knead it until it is soft and pliable. Cover the dough with a well-moistened cloth and keep aside for ½-1 hour.

2. Hand Method: Put the flour and salt in a large bowl and rub in the fat. Gradually add the water, and keep mixing and kneading until a soft and pliable dough is formed. Cover the dough as above and keep aside.

3. Divide the dough into 14 walnut-sized portions. Roll each portion in a circular motion between the palms to make a smooth round

Step 3 Roll each portion of dough in a circular motion between the palms to make a smooth, round ball.

ball, then flatten the ball to make a round cake. Dip each cake into the dry flour and roll the chapatti into a disc of about 6-inch diameter.

4. An iron griddle is normally used for cooking chapatties, but if you do not have one, use a heavy-based skillet as the chapatties need even distribution of heat during cooking. Overheating of the pan will cause the chapatties to stick and burn.

5. Heat the griddle or skillet over medium heat and place a chapatti on it. Cook 30 seconds and turn the chapatti over. Cook until brown spots appear on both sides, turning it over frequently.

6. To keep the chapatties warm, line a piece of aluminum foil with absorbent paper and place the chapatties on one end. Cover with the other end and seal the edges.

Tandoori Roti

MAKES 8

Tandoori Rotis, like chapatties, can be served with any meat, chicken, or vegetable curry.

PREPARATION: 10-15 mins
COOKING: 25 mins

⅔ cup plain yogurt
4 cups all-purpose flour
1 tsp sugar
1 tsp baking powder
½ tsp salt
1 package active dry yeast
1 level tbsp ghee or unsalted butter
1 medium egg, beaten
⅔ cup warm milk

1. Beat the yogurt until smooth, and set aside.

2. In a large bowl, sift the flour with the sugar, baking powder, salt, and yeast. Add ghee and mix thoroughly. Add yogurt and egg and knead well.

Step 3
Gradually add the warm milk, and keep kneading until a smooth, springy dough is formed.

3. Gradually add the warm milk and keep kneading until a smooth and springy dough is formed.

4. Place the dough in a large plastic food bag and tie up the uppermost part of the bag so that the dough has enough room for expansion inside.

5. Rinse a large bowl with hot water and put the bag of dough in it. Use a steel, metal, or enamel bowl as these will retain heat better. Place the bowl in a warm place for ½-¾ hour when it will be almost double in volume.

6. Preheat oven to 450°F.

7. Line a baking tray with greased parchment paper or nonstick baking paper.

8. Divide the dough into 8 equal-sized balls. Place a ball between your palms and flatten by pressing it down.

9. Dust the ball lightly in a little flour and roll it out gently to a 4-inch disk. Place in the prepared baking tray. Make the rest of the rotis the same way.

10. Bake on the top shelf of the oven 10-12 minutes. Turn the rotis over and bake for a further 2 minutes.

Mattar Pilau

SERVES 4-6

An easy to prepare pilau rice which has an attractive look provided by the rich green color of the garden peas.

PREPARATION: 10 mins, plus time needed to soak the rice

COOKING: 25-30 mins

1¼ cups basmati or long grain rice
⅓ cup ghee (clarified butter) or unsalted butter
2 tsps fennel seeds
2-3 dried red chilies
6 whole cloves
2 cinnamon sticks, 2-inches long each, broken up
6 green cardamoms, split open the top of each pod
2 bayleaves, crumbled
1 large onion, finely sliced
¾ cup frozen garden peas
1 tsp ground turmeric
1¼ tsps salt
2½ cups water

Step 2 Melt the butter over medium heat and fry the fennel seeds until they are brown.

Step 4 Add the rice, peas, turmeric, and salt. Stir and fry until the rice is fairly dry.

1. Wash the rice and soak it in cold water half an hour. Drain thoroughly.

2. Melt the butter over medium heat and sauté the fennel seeds until they are brown.

3. Add the chilies, cloves, cinnamon, cardamom, and bayleaves. Stir once and add the onions. Sauté until the onions are lightly browned, stirring frequently.

4. Add the rice, peas, turmeric, and salt. Stir and fry for 4-5 minutes until the rice is fairly dry, lowering heat towards the last 1-2 minutes.

5. Add the water and bring to the boil. Cover the pan and simmer 12-15 minutes without lifting the lid. Remove the pan from heat and leave it undisturbed for a further 10-15 minutes. Remove the cinnamon, cardamom pods, and bayleaves before serving.

Fried Brown Rice

SERVES 4-6

This traditional rice dish complements Fish Shahjahani perfectly.

PREPARATION: time needed to soak the rice
COOKING: 20-25 mins

1¼ cups basmati or other long grain rice
4 tbsps oil
4 tsps sugar
1 tsp cumin seeds
2 cinnamon sticks, 2-inch long each, broken up
6 whole cloves
6 black peppercorns
2 bayleaves, crumbled
2½ cups water
1 tsp salt

1. Wash the rice and soak in cold water for 30 minutes. Drain well.

2. In a heavy-based saucepan, heat the oil over medium heat and add the sugar.

3. The sugar will gradually begin to change color to a dark brown. As soon as it does, add the cumin seeds, cinnamon, cloves, black peppercorns, and bayleaves. Fry for 30 seconds.

4. Add the rice and fry about 5 minutes, stirring frequently and lowering heat for the last minute or two.

5. Add the water and salt. Bring to the boil,

Step 1 Wash the rice and soak in cold water for 30 minutes.

cover and simmer without lifting the lid. Cooking time will be 12-15 minutes for basmati rice, 15-18 minutes for other long grain rice.

6. Remove the pan from heat and keep it undisturbed for a further 10-15 minutes before serving. Remove the cinnamon and bayleaves before serving.

Step 3 As the sugar changes color to dark brown add the cumin seeds, cinnamon, cloves, black peppercorns, and bayleaves.

Tarka Dhal
(Spiced Lentils)

SERVES 4

Dhal is a good source of protein and dhal of some sort is always cooked as part of a meal in an Indian household.

PREPARATION: 10 mins
COOKING: 50 mins

¾ cup Masoor dhal (red split lentils)
3¼ cups water
1 tsp ground turmeric
1 tsp ground cumin
1 tsp salt
2 tbsps ghee (clarified butter) or unsalted butter
1 medium-sized onion, minced
2 cloves garlic, peeled and minced
2 dried red chilies, coarsely chopped

---

1. Put the dhal, water, turmeric, cumin, and salt into a saucepan and bring the liquid to the boil.

Step 2 Reduce heat to medium and cook uncovered 8-10 minutes, stirring frequently.

Step 4 Remove the dhal from the heat, allow to cool slightly, and mash through a sieve.

2. Reduce heat to medium and cook uncovered 8-10 minutes, stirring frequently.

3. Now cover the pan and simmer 30 minutes, stirring occasionally.

4. Remove the dhal from the heat, allow to cool slightly and mash through a sieve.

5. Melt the ghee or butter over medium heat and fry the onion, garlic, and red chilies until the onions are well browned.

6. Stir in half the fried onion mixture to the dhal and put the dhal in a serving dish. Arrange the remaining fried onions on top.

Cauliflower Masala

SERVES 4-6

This dish is flavored with a few basic ingredients and the finished dish is semi-dry, making it an ideal accompaniment to rice and curry or Indian bread.

PREPARATION: 25 mins
COOKING: 30-35 mins

1 medium-sized cauliflower
2 medium-sized potatoes
4 tbsps cooking oil
1 tsp cumin seeds
1 large onion
½ tsp ground turmeric
1 tsp ground coriander
1 tsp ground cumin
¼-½ tsp chili powder
2 ripe tomatoes, skinned and chopped
¾ cup warm water
½ cup frozen peas
1-2 fresh green chilies, seeded and slit
    lengthwise into halves
1 tsp salt
½ tsp garam masala
1 tbsp chopped coriander (cilantro) leaves

1. Cut the cauliflower into flowerets. Wash and drain.

2. Peel and cut the potatoes lengthwise into strips about ½-inch thick.

3. Heat the oil over medium heat and add the cumin seeds. As soon as they start popping,

Step 3 As soon as the cumin seeds start popping, add the onions and sauté until they are soft.

add the onions and fry until they are soft.

4. Turn heat down to low and add the turmeric, coriander, cumin, and chili powder. Stir and fry 2-3 minutes and add the chopped tomatoes. Fry a further 2-3 minutes stirring continuously.

5. Add the potatoes and the water. Bring to the boil, cover the pan, and simmer until the potatoes are half-cooked.

6. Add the cauliflower, cover the pan again, and simmer for 10 minutes until the potatoes are tender.

7. Stir in the peas, green chilies, salt, and garam masala. Cover and cook 5 minutes.

8. Remove from heat and stir in the coriander leaves.

Aloo Mattar

SERVES 4-6

Aloo Mattar is a semi-moist potato dish which blends easily with meat, chicken or fish curries.

PREPARATION: 10-15 mins
COOKING: 25-30 mins

---

4 tbsps cooking oil
1 medium-sized onion, finely chopped
2 cinnamon sticks, each 2-inches long, broken up
½-inch root ginger, peeled and finely chopped
½ tsp ground turmeric
2 tsps ground cumin
¼ tsp chili powder
¼ tsp freshly ground black pepper
1 pound potatoes, peeled and cut into 1-inch cubes
1-2 whole fresh green chilies
1 tbsp tomato paste
1 tsp salt
1 cup warm water
½ cup frozen garden peas
1 tbsp chopped coriander (cilantro) leaves

---

1. Heat the oil over medium heat and fry the onion, cinnamon, and ginger 4-5 minutes, stirring frequently.

2. Reduce heat to low and add the turmeric,

Step 3 Add the potatoes and the green chilies, stir and cook until the spices are blended thoroughly.

cumin, chili powder, and black pepper. Stir and fry one minute.

3. Add the potatoes and the green chilies, stir and cook until the spices are blended thoroughly (2-3 minutes).

4. Stir in the tomato paste and salt.

5. Add the water, bring to the boil, cover the pan, and cook over medium to low heat 10 minutes until the potatoes are half-cooked.

6. Add the peas, cover the pan and cook until the potatoes are tender.

7. Remove the pan from the heat, stir in half the coriander leaves (if used), and sprinkle the remainder on top.

Gobi Mattar
(Cabbage with Garden Peas)

SERVES 4-6

This quick and easy side dish is the ideal accompaniment for Meat Madras.

PREPARATION: 15 mins
COOKING: 10-15 mins

---

12 ounces green cabbage
3 tbsps cooking oil
¼ tsp black mustard seeds
½ tsp cumin seeds
10-12 fenugreek seeds (optional)
2-4 whole dried red chilies
1 small onion, finely sliced
½ tsp ground turmeric
½ cup frozen garden peas
¾ tsp salt
1 tsp ground coriander
¼-½ tsp chili powder
2 small ripe tomatoes, skinned and chopped
1 tbsp chopped coriander (cilantro) leaves

---

1. Shred or chop the cabbage finely.

Step 1 Shred or chop the cabbage finely.

Step 6 Add the ground coriander, the chili powder, and the chopped tomatoes.

2. Heat the oil over medium heat and sauté the mustard seeds until they pop.

3. Add the cumin seeds followed by the fenugreek (if used), red chilies, and the onions. Stir and fry until the onions are soft.

4. Stir in the turmeric and add the cabbage. Stir and mix thoroughly.

5. Add the peas and salt, stir and cover the pan. Lower heat to minimum and cook 5 minutes.

6. Add the ground coriander, the chili powder, and the chopped tomatoes. Stir until the mixture is completely dry.

7. Remove from heat and stir in half the coriander leaves.

8. Put the cabbage into a serving dish and sprinkle the remaining coriander leaves on top.

Tomato and Cucumber Salad

SERVES 4-6

This salad, with its combination of cucumber, tomato and roasted peanuts makes a mouthwatering side dish.

PREPARATION: 10 mins

1 cucumber
2 tomatoes
1 bunch green onions (scallions), chopped
1 tbsp lemon juice
1 tbsp olive oil
¼ tsp salt
¼ tsp freshly ground black pepper
1 tbsp chopped coriander (cilantro) leaves
2 tbsps roasted salted peanuts, crushed

Step 4 Combine the lemon juice, olive oil, salt, pepper, and coriander leaves, and keep aside.

Step 3 Put the cucumber, tomatoes, and green onions into a serving bowl.

1. Peel the cucumber and chop finely.

2. Chop the tomatoes finely.

3. Put cucumber, tomatoes, and green onions into a serving bowl.

4. Combine the lemon juice, olive oil, salt, pepper, and coriander leaves and keep aside.

5. Just before serving, stir in the peanuts and the dressing.

Index

Meat Madras, a hot curry from southern India